CREEPY CREATURES

Sneed B. Collard III • Illustrated by Kristin Kest

ini Charlesbridge

One World — S.B.C.

For Kira Peikoff — K.K.

Text and illustrations copyright © 1992 by Charlesbridge Publishing
Cover design copyright © 1997 by Charlesbridge Publishing
Library of Congress Cataloging-in-Publication Data is available upon request.
ISBN 0-88106-837-3 (reinforced for library use)
ISBN 0-88106-836-5 (softcover)
Published by Charlesbridge Publishing, 85 Main Street, Watertown, MA 02472 • (617) 926-0329
www.charlesbridge.com

Printed in the United States of America
(hc) 10 9 8 7 6 5 4 3 2 1
(sc) 10 9 8 7 6 5 4 3 2

Earth is home to millions of different creatures. Some of them please us. Some frighten us. Others make us say "Blech!" Yet no matter how we feel about it, each animal is special.

At first, you might think this book is filled with scary, creepy creatures. But each animal's scary looks or habits serve a purpose. They allow the animal to live in its own special way and place.

Are the animals in this book really scary? Turn the page to find out.

SHARKS

Sharks don't cry, but they are sensitive. Sensitive eyes
help them see in very bright and very dim light.
Sharks can sense other animals moving in
the water hundreds of feet away. Sharks
are so sensitive they can even feel
tiny currents of electricity
in the water.

A shark's
senses help
make it a skilled
hunter. This sand
tiger shark eats mostly
crabs and small fish.

Sharks don't seem to like
the taste of people very much.
People, on the other hand, eat
millions of shark steaks each year.
Maybe sharks should be afraid of us!

PANGOLINS

Pangolins are not
leftover dinosaurs, or funny
looking lizards. They are more like anteaters with scales. Like anteaters, they slurp
up insects with their long, sticky tongues. A pangolin's scales protect it from the
bites of insects and bigger animals. When it is scared, a pangolin rolls into a tight
ball. Unrolling a pangolin is like peeling a rock — it is almost impossible!

TARANTULAS

Imagine watching TV with a tarantula! In some South American homes, pet tarantulas are allowed to walk around eating harmful insects and small animals.

Tarantula venom is not usually dangerous to people. Tarantulas use their venom to kill and digest their prey. Without tarantulas and other spiders, we might soon be swimming in a sea of insects!

SPOTTED HYENAS

Suddenly the silence of the African night is broken by a horrible, high-pitched laugh. Hyenas are on the prowl. Like lions, hyenas live and hunt in groups. Hyenas may laugh around the dinner table, but there is nothing funny going on. Laughing is a hyena's way of talking to the other hyenas in its family.

PIRANHAS

A piranha that is being pulled out of the water may snap off a fisherman's finger with its razor-sharp teeth. In the water, however, piranhas rarely attack anything larger than a frog. These South American fish think a tasty meal includes crabs, other fish, fruit, seeds, and even flowers. Only in myths and movies are piranhas always dangerous.

BATS

Bats get
their bad
name from scary stories about imaginary creatures called vampires.
There are vampire bats that drink the blood of cattle, but even they are helpful. Doctors
are studying them to find a cure for people who have blood clots and heart attacks.

Bats are the only mammals that can fly.

Bats are important because they help control insects.

One bat can eat 600 mosquitos in an hour. In Asia and Africa, giant fruit-eating bats called flying foxes spread the seeds of rain forest trees. Many night-flowering trees, bushes, and cactuses would die out without bats to pollinate them.

VULTURES

The vulture would never win a beauty contest, but it's a very good garbage disposal. It eats animals that have died or been killed by others. A vulture can soar high up in the sky for hours. When its sharp eyes spot a dead animal, the bird swoops down for a meal.

The vulture's bald head may look strange, but it is practical. Head feathers would just get in the way when the vulture is eating a messy carcass.

PYTHONS

Pythons are the world's longest snakes, sometimes over 30 feet long! An adult python thinks a chicken, duck, or guinea pig is a nice snack, but it can go for months without eating at all.

Pythons use their powerful muscles to hold their prey so tightly that it cannot breathe. A python can raise its own body temperature by tightening its muscles as if it were shivering. This is how a female python keeps her eggs warm until they hatch.

MORAY EELS

Moray eels would make terrible movie stars. Most hide shyly in rocks or coral reefs. Morays look like they're about to bite, but that's because they must keep their mouths open to breathe. A moray usually does not attack unless a diver sticks a hand into its hole. The nearsighted moray apparently thinks the diver's hand looks like a little octopus — the moray's favorite meal.

STAR-NOSED MOLES

You're not likely to meet a star-nosed mole unless you're underground. With its big front feet, the star-nosed mole swims through the soil. This one has just caught an earthworm. It doesn't have much use for eyes.   Instead, the star-nosed mole finds its food with the 22 fingerlike tentacles around its nose. Imagine learning to count with 22 fingers!

KOMODO DRAGONS

Komodo dragons or "oras" are the world's largest lizards. Oras grow to ten feet long from snout to tail. Experts believe oras live as long as fifty years, but no one is sure. There's no good way to tell an ora's age, and these lizards never hold birthday parties.

An ora's enormous size lets it catch and eat everything from grasshoppers to goats. Oras use their tongues to smell food, and their sense of smell is excellent. Don't worry though, oras usually run away when they smell a human being — and they will smell you only if you go to one of the six tiny islands in Indonesia where they live.

ELECTRIC RAYS

ZAP! Fish get a real charge out of an electric ray. This ray silently glides over a sleeping fish and then stuns it with a jolt of electricity. Afterward, the ray does a somersault over its stunned prey. Its somersault is not a jump for joy. The somersault helps the ray swallow its meal.

SCORPIONS

Scorpions are not friendly, but they will not attack you either.
Many scorpions live in burrows that they dig with their
claws, legs, and tails. Once it moves into its burrow,
a scorpion spends most of its time there.

Underground,
the scorpion
is safe from
the hot sun and
from being eaten by birds, lizards, and other predators.
A scorpion uses the stinger on its tail to protect itself from
bigger animals and to paralyze the insects and spiders that it eats.

TASMANIAN DEVILS

If you see a Tasmanian devil with red ears, watch out! When it is cornered, this marsupial snorts, spits, screeches, and snarls like a huge monster. It's really just a small, shy animal with a pouch like a kangaroo.

Tasmanian devils eat mammals, birds, lizards, and insects, but they like to stay clean. After they eat, they wash their hands and give their faces a good scrubbing. There is nothing a Tasmanian devil likes better than taking a bath and then basking in the warm sun.

PORTUGUESE MAN-OF-WAR

Wherever the wind blows, the Portuguese Man-of-War sails along with it. The balloon-like sail of this jellyfish is filled with gas that keeps it afloat. The Man-of-War uses its tentacles to sting and capture its prey. Yet one kind of fish never gets stung. It is called the nomeus or the Portuguese Man-of-War fish. The jellyfish is a floating fortress for the little fish, keeping it safe from its hungry enemies.

GIANT
SQUID
It's as long as two school
buses, and has eyes the size
of dinner plates. Its 8 arms and 2
tentacles grow right out of its head. Is
the giant squid from another planet? No, but
it does live thousands of feet deep in the ocean.

The giant squid eats fish and smaller squids. To escape sperm whales and other enemies, the giant squid can squirt out a confusing cloud of black ink. Giant squids also respond to danger by changing their color in a flash. Scientists are studying squid nervous systems to help them learn how human nerves work.

GULPERS and VIPER FISH

Like the giant squid, gulpers and viper fish live deep in the ocean where it's very dark. They attract their prey with lights on their bodies. When a curious creature comes close to a gulper's glowing tail — GULP! The animal is gulped right down. With their huge jaws, gulpers and viper fish can swallow animals bigger than themselves. With a mouth that size, who needs a lunchbox?

GOLIATH BEETLES

It's a can   opener. . . . It's an armored car. . . . No, it's a goliath beetle!
Over six inches long, goliath beetles look as if they could never get off the ground. Yet
their wings are larger than a sparrow's. They are good fliers, making a loud whirring
noise as they zip by. In Africa, children spend hours playing with these huge insects.

LEECHES

Leeches are not
the heroes of any stories,
but they are not the bad
guys either. These distant
cousins of the earthworm
live in swampy places. Some
leeches suck blood, but leech
bites don't hurt. That's because
leeches make pain
killers so
animals won't
know
they've
been
bitten.

Doctors use these pain killers and many other
"leechy" chemicals to help sick people get better.

WARTHOGS

Warthogs are one of the most unpredictable animals on the African plains. Usually they are peaceful. They spend up to half of their day kneeling down to get close enough to the ground to munch grass.

When they are startled or frightened, however, they will charge at their enemies and slash at them with their long, canine teeth. Sharp teeth, speed, and a bad reputation are their defenses against wild dogs, lions, and leopards. No one knows why warthogs have those strange growths or warts. They probably protect the warthog's eyes and jaws during a fight.

SPIDER CRABS

The spider crab looks like a spider gone wild. It scuttles over the sea floor on its five pairs of legs. The spider crab's extra-long front legs have pincers for grabbing shellfish and plants to eat. Spider crabs decorate themselves by putting live seaweed and sponges on their shells. Sharks and other hunters can't see a spider crab as well when it is wearing this disguise.

RAZOR-TOOTH SLIME-ENCRUSTED BONE MUNCHERS

Razor-tooth slime-encrusted bone munchers are terrible, disgusting creatures. They kill anything, and then they sing and dance around their unfortunate victims. The way they kill is truly horrifying.

When you're not looking, they creep up behind you.

Then, they drip slime over you until — well, you know.

It's a good thing . . .

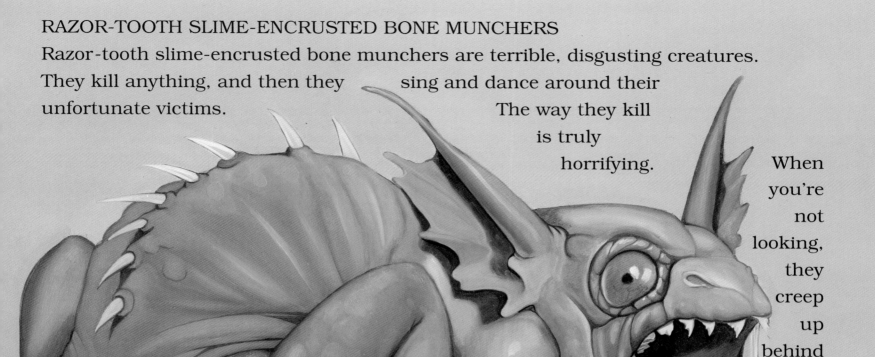

nothing like a razor-tooth slime-encrusted bone muncher exists!

In fact, no animal exists just to scare, hurt, or disgust us. To live in the world, each creature needs to find food and defend itself. It needs to have a home and find its way around. Understanding how an animal does these things helps us learn how very special each creature is. For no matter how scary it seems to us at first, each creature depends on its own special claws, tentacles, stingers, teeth, scales, size, and habits to survive.

Do they scare you? Now, you know that there's no reason to be scared.

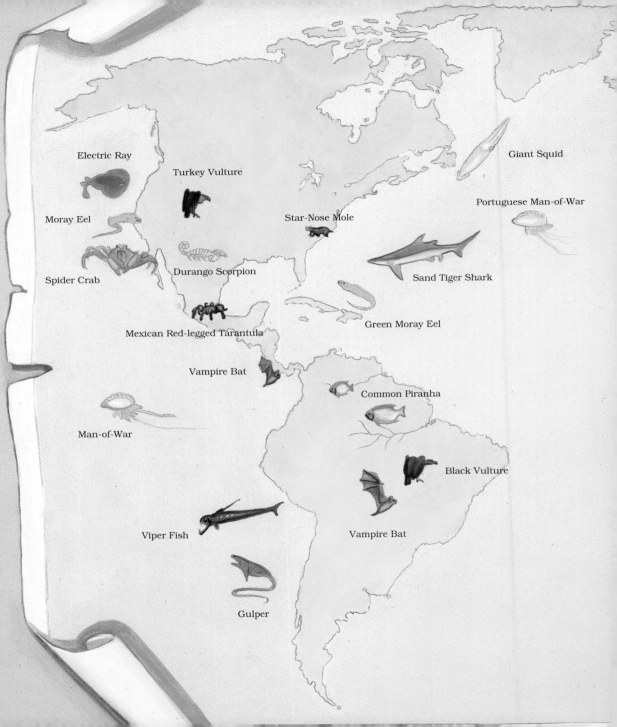

Electric Ray

Turkey Vulture

Giant Squid

Portuguese Man-of-War

Moray Eel

Star-Nose Mole

Spider Crab

Durango Scorpion

Sand Tiger Shark

Green Moray Eel

Mexican Red-legged Tarantula

Vampire Bat

Common Piranha

Man-of-War

Black Vulture

Viper Fish

Vampire Bat

Gulper

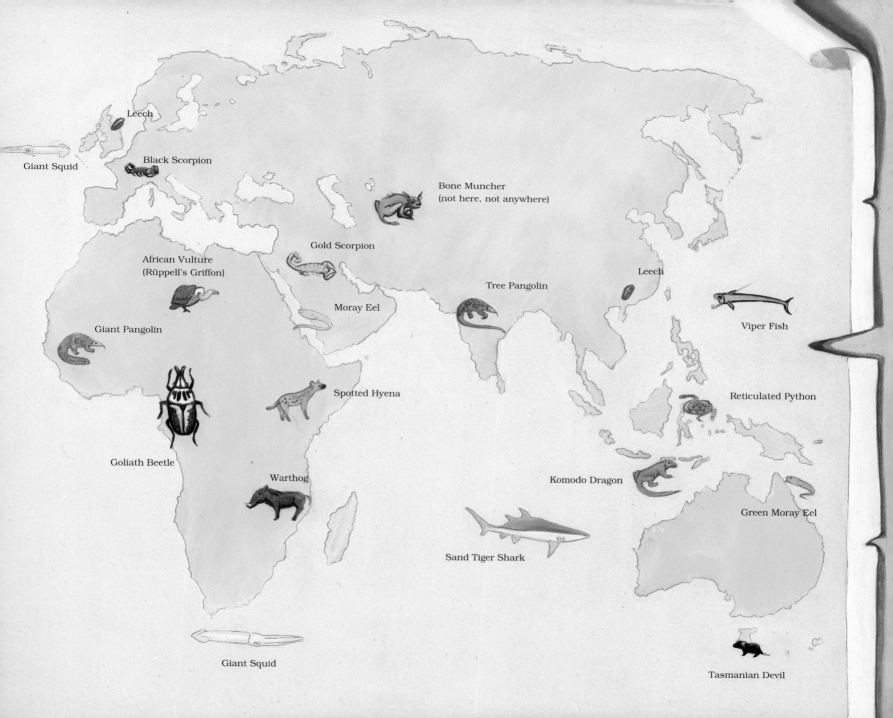

Leech

Giant Squid

Black Scorpion

Bone Muncher
(not here, not anywhere)

Gold Scorpion

African Vulture
(Rüppell's Griffon)

Moray Eel

Tree Pangolin

Leech

Viper Fish

Giant Pangolin

Spotted Hyena

Reticulated Python

Goliath Beetle

Warthog

Komodo Dragon

Green Moray Eel

Sand Tiger Shark

Giant Squid

Tasmanian Devil